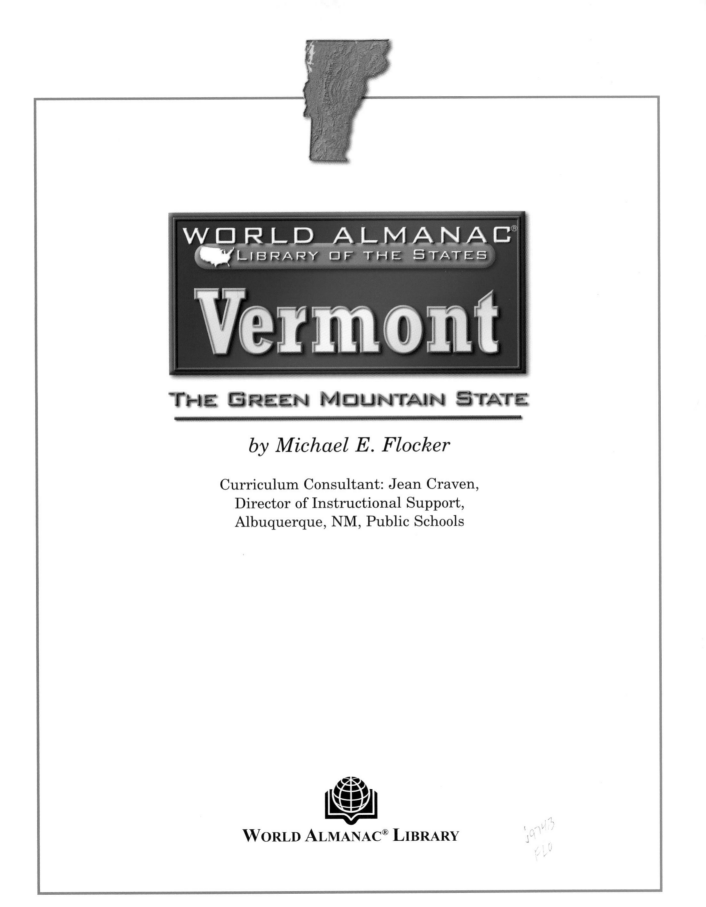

WORLD ALMANAC®
LIBRARY OF THE STATES

Vermont

THE GREEN MOUNTAIN STATE

by Michael E. Flocker

Curriculum Consultant: Jean Craven,
Director of Instructional Support,
Albuquerque, NM, Public Schools

WORLD ALMANAC® LIBRARY

Please visit our web site at: **www.worldalmanaclibrary.com**
For a free color catalog describing World Almanac® Library's
list of high-quality books and multimedia programs, call
1-800-848-2928 (USA) or 1-800-387-3178 (Canada).
World Almanac® Library's fax: (414) 332-3567.

Library of Congress Cataloging-in-Publication Data

Flocker, Michael.
    Vermont, the Green Mountain State / by Michael Flocker.
       p. cm. — (World Almanac Library of the states)
    Includes bibliographical references and index.
    Summary: Surveys the history, land, economy, politics and government,
culture, and notable people and events of Vermont.
    ISBN 0-8368-5146-3 (lib. bdg.)
    ISBN 0-8368-5316-4 (softcover)
    1. Vermont—Juvenile literature. [1. Vermont.] I. Title. II. Series.
F49.3.F57   2002
974.3—dc21   2002023485

This edition first published in 2002 by
World Almanac® Library
330 West Olive Street, Suite 100
Milwaukee, WI 53212 USA

This edition © 2002 by World Almanac® Library.

Design and Editorial: Bill SMITH STUDIO Inc.
Editor: Kristen Behrens
Assistant Editor: Megan Elias
Art Director: Jay Jaffe
Photo Research: Sean Livingstone
World Almanac® Library Project Editor: Patricia Lantier
World Almanac® Library Editors: Jacqueline Laks Gorman, Monica Rausch
World Almanac® Library Production: Scott M. Krall, Tammy Gruenewald,
  Katherine A. Goedheer

Photo credits: p. 4 © PhotoDisc; p. 6 (all) © Corel; p. 7 (top) © Brattleboro, (bottom) © PAINET
INC.; p. 9 © Bettmann/CORBIS; p. 10 Dover; p. 11 © ArtToday; p. 12 © Bettmann/CORBIS; p. 13
© Margaret Bourke-White/TimePix; pp. 14-15 © Library of Congress; p. 17 ©James P.
Blair/CORBIS; p. 18 © Library of Congress; p. 19 VT Dept. of Tourism; p. 20 (left to right)
© PAINET INC., © Corel, © Corel; p. 21 (left to right) © Corel, © Corel, Vermont Dept. of Tourism;
p. 23 © Corel; p. 26 (top) © Corel, (bottom) © PhotoDisc; p. 27 © PhotoDisc; p. 29 Vermont Dept.
of Tourism; p. 31 (left) © Library of Congress, (right) © Library of Congress, (bottom)
© Jim Bourg/Reuters/TimePix; p. 32 © PhotoDisc; p. 33 VT Dept. of Tourism; p. 34 © James P.
Blair/CORBIS; p. 35 (inset) © Corel, (bottom) © PhotoDisc; p. 36 (top) VT Dept. of Tourism,
(bottom) © PAINET INC.; p. 37 Vermont Dept. of Tourism; p. 38 Dover; p. 39 (top right) Dover,
p. 39 (bottom left) © Corel; p. 40 © PhotoDisc; p. 41 © Cornelis Verwaal/TimePix; p. 42-43
© Library of Congress; p. 44 (left) © PhotoSpin, (bottom) © Artville; p. 45 (top) © PhotoDisc,
(bottom right) © ArtToday.

Printed in the United States of America

1 2 3 4 5 6 7 8 9 06 05 04 03 02

Vermont

A State of Independence

Postcard-perfect images of woods ablaze with fall colors, lush pastures dotted with grazing cattle, quaint town greens with white steepled churches, and snowy forested slopes all say "Vermont," but there is more to learn about the state.

It took several ice ages to form the landscape that today features mountain ranges, fertile valleys, lakes, and rivers. For thousands of years, the area was home to Native peoples who first hunted, then cultivated the land. The French were the first Europeans to visit the region. Although they did not establish permanent settlements, their legacy is evident in place names such as Lake Champlain, Calais, Montpelier, and even Vermont itself. The British followed the French into Vermont and in the early eighteenth century succeeded in founding a permanent settlement. The rest of the century was marked by conflict — first between the French and the British, then between two British colonies over which would control Vermont. When the Revolutionary War broke out, Vermonters declared themselves an independent republic, adopting a constitution that outlawed slavery, expanded voting rights, and established schools. Vermont's independent streak remained even after it joined the Union, and it continues today.

Vermonters are connected to the land. Until the twentieth century, when manufacturing took a leading role, farming was the most important source of income. In the late twentieth century, a new industry — tourism — gave Vermonters another reason to care for the state's environment. Millions of visitors are drawn to Vermont's ski resorts, state parks, and historic sites. With shrewd foresight and careful planning, the people of Vermont are working to preserve their state's beauty and rural charm for the generations to come.

► Map of Vermont showing the interstate highway system, as well as major cities and waterways.

▼ Vermont's fall foliage draws tourists from around the world.

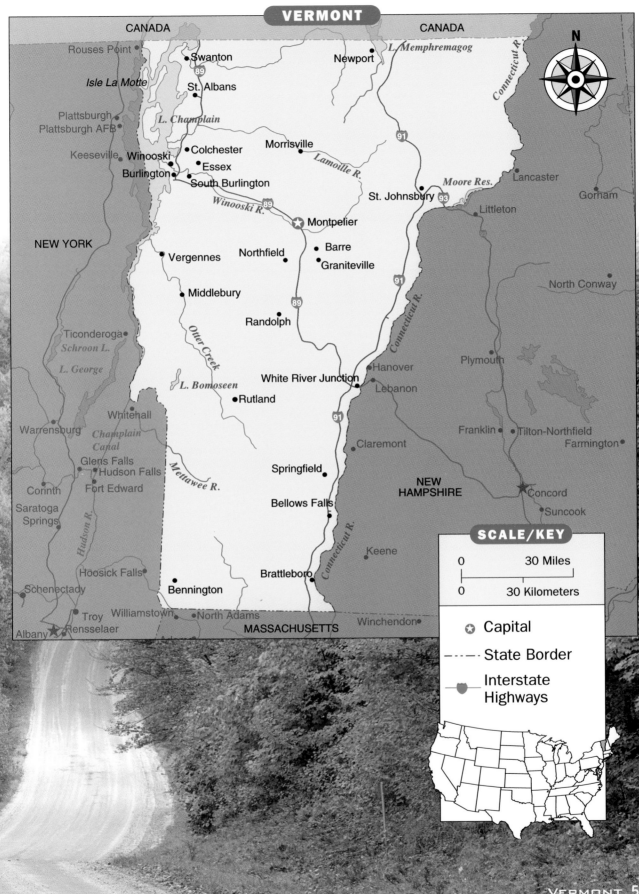

VERMONT

CANADA

CANADA

Rouses Point

• Swanton

Newport

L. Memphremagog

89

St. Albans

Isle La Motte

Connecticut R.

Plattsburgh

Plattsburgh AFB

L. Champlain

Morrisville

91

Keeseville

Winooski

• Colchester

Lamoille R.

Moore Res.

Lancaster

• Essex

Burlington

St. Johnsbury

Littleton

South Burlington

93

Gorham

Winooski R.

89

☆ Montpelier

NEW YORK

• Barre

Vergennes

Northfield

• Graniteville

North Conway

91

Middlebury

Connecticut R.

Otter Creek

Randolph

Ticonderoga

Schroon L.

Plymouth

L. George

L. Bomoseen

White River Junction

• Hanover

Warrensburg

Rutland

Lebanon

Champlain Canal

Franklin

• Tilton-Northfield

Whitehall

Farmington

Glens Falls

Claremont

Hudson Falls

91

Corinth

Fort Edward

Mettawee R.

Springfield

NEW HAMPSHIRE

Concord

Saratoga Springs

Hudson R.

Bellows Falls

Suncook

Hoosick Falls

Keene

Brattleboro

Connecticut R.

Schenectady

Bennington

Troy

Williamstown

North Adams

Winchendon

Albany

Rensselaer

MASSACHUSETTS

SCALE/KEY

0   30 Miles

0   30 Kilometers

✪ Capital

––·––· State Border

Interstate Highways

Fast Facts

VERMONT (VT), The Green Mountain State

Entered Union
March 4, 1791 (14th state)

Capital
Montpelier 8,035

Population

Total Population (2000)
608,827 (49th most populous state) — *Between 1990 and 2000, population of Vermont increased by 8.2 percent.*

Largest Cities or Towns — Population
Burlington 38,889
Essex 18,626
Rutland 17,292
Colchester 16,986
South Burlington 15,814

Land Area
9,250 square miles (23,958 square kilometers) (43rd largest state)

State Motto
"Freedom and Unity"

State Song
"These Green Mountains" *by Diane Martin, arranged by Rita Buglass, adopted in 2000*

State Animal
Morgan horse

State Bird
Hermit thrush — *Known for its distinctive, sweet call, the hermit thrush leaves Vermont each winter and heads south.*

State Insect
Honeybee — *Aside from pollinating a variety of crops, Vermont honeybees also produce hundreds of thousands of pounds of honey each year.*

State Tree
Sugar maple — *During late winter and early spring, the sap drawn from these trees is boiled down to produce the state's famous pancake topping.*

State Flower
Red clover — *Brought to North America by English colonists, it provides nectar for Vermont honeybees, forage for Vermont cattle, and nutrients for the soil in which it grows.*

State Butterfly
Monarch butterfly — *Also known as Danaus plexippus.*

State Gem
Grossular garnet — *Because of the presence of iron in its chemical composition, the grossular garnet is brown.*

State Fruit
Apple — *Over $14 million worth of apples are produced in Vermont each year and sold throughout the world.*

Ben & Jerry's Ice Cream Factory, *Waterbury*
A factory tour starts with a seven-minute film about the company's founding, continues with a tour of the factory, and ends with free samples. In winter, the factory also offers snowshoe tours of the area.

Ethan Allen Homestead, *Burlington*
This historic site and museum features the 1787 farmhouse that was the last home of Ethan Allen, Revolutionary War hero and Vermont founder. Visitors can also view exhibits about colonial and Vermont history.

Green Mountain National Forest
Covering more than 350,000 acres (141,645 hectares), the forest offers opportunities for hiking, cross-country skiing, snowmobiling, and fishing. There are 312 miles (502 km) of trails as well as camping and picnic areas.

For other places and events, see p. 44.

BIGGEST, BEST, AND MOST

- Vermont is the national leader in maple syrup production.

STATE FIRSTS

- **1777** The Vermont Constitution was the first in North America to outlaw slavery and the first to guarantee voting rights to all men.
- **1783** Lemuel Haynes became the first African-American pastor of a white congregation.
- **1791** Vermont was the first state to be admitted to the Union after the ratification of the U.S. Constitution.
- **1814** Emma Hart Willard opened the first U.S. school for the higher education of women in her home in Middlebury.
- **1940** Ida May Fuller of Ludlow was the first person to receive a Social Security check.

Got Mail?

British writer Rudyard Kipling moved to Dummerston in 1892. During the next four years, he wrote some of his most popular works, including *The Jungle Book*. To avoid curious townspeople, Kipling began receiving his mail in Brattleboro. By 1895, he got more mail than Brattleboro's largest business. The U.S. postmaster general authorized a special post office to be set up in the home of Kipling's neighbor, Anna F. Waite. Waite was then appointed the office's postmistress. The office only accepted letters addressed to Kipling's household. Today, philatelists, or stamp collectors, prize the Waite postmark because it was from the first — and last — post office to be set up for one person. The post office lasted for just two years. The Kiplings left Vermont in 1896, and the post office closed in 1897.

Please note change of Address:
BRATTLEBORO, VT.
TO WAITE.
Windham County,
Careful not to omit name of County.
Vermont.
Rudyard Kipling

Justin Morgan Had a Horse

In 1789, music teacher and businessman Justin Morgan of Randolph accepted a horse in payment of a debt he was owed. The stallion, called Figure, performed amazing feats of strength and won renown throughout the area. When Justin Morgan died, the horse passed to other owners. Over the years, Figure came to be known as "Justin Morgan's Horse." Farmers used his offspring to develop a new breed known as the Morgan. In turn, the Morgan contributed its bloodlines to other U.S. horse breeds, including the quarter horse, the saddlebred, the standardbred, and the Tennessee walking horse.

▶ **A modern Morgan horse shows off its paces.**

Forging a People

> (Vermonters are) a peculiar folk whom the very word Freedom
> and its implications made a little drunk. Freedom had come up
> over the border with them into the new land. In a strange way,
> the climate, the soil, the contours of the land itself, had
> nurtured — still preserves — that disconcerting passion.
>
> — *Frederic Van de Water,* The Reluctant Republic:
> Vermont 1724–1791, *1941*

Archaeologists believe that humans have lived in the area now called Vermont for as many as nine thousand years. The earliest inhabitants probably were nomadic and hunted big game for food. Over thousands of years, the ecosystem changed. Native people began fishing, gathering plant foods, and hunting smaller game. Later, they established settlements, made pottery and bows and arrows, and began farming. By the time European explorers arrived, two Native cultures lived on the land: the Iroquois and the Algonquian. Eventually, most Iroquois moved west, toward New York. The Algonquian-speaking Abenaki stayed in Vermont, living near the lakes and rivers to hunt, fish, and farm in the warmer seasons and moving to higher ground, where game was more plentiful, in winter.

Native Americans of Vermont
Abenaki
Iroquois
Mohican
Narragansett
Pennacook
Pocumtuc
Wampanoag

Enter the Europeans

In 1609, French explorer Samuel de Champlain left the town of Quebec, Canada (which he had founded the year before) to explore the area to his south. On the way, he came upon the lake that now bears his name. Along the lake's eastern shore he saw mountains that he called *Les Monts Verts* — French for "the Green Mountains." Champlain is the first European known to have visited the region. Over time, he formed an alliance with the Abenaki and helped them in their struggles to protect their lands from other Native Americans, including the Iroquois who made frequent raids. Champlain eventually claimed the land for his native France.

It wasn't until 1666 that the first European settlement was established. Fort Ste. Anne was built on the Isle La Motte in Lake Champlain. Other French military posts were also established, but none of them proved permanent. For many years, Vermont served mainly as a thoroughfare among British, French, and Native American settlements.

Colonial Tensions

From the time Fort Ste. Anne was built until 1763, the French sporadically battled with both the Iroquois and the British for control of the region. British colonists began moving north from Connecticut, Massachusetts, New York, and New Hampshire, and Vermont's first permanent English-speaking settlement was established in 1724 at Fort Dummer — present-day Brattleboro. Eventually, more and more English-speaking settlers arrived, all of whom attempted to claim the Vermont region for their home colony. Tensions between these settlers and the French grew.

Both the British and the French vied to establish alliances with the local Native Americans. With the outbreak of the French and Indian War in 1754, the French sided with the Abenaki and the British joined forces with the Iroquois as each side struggled to gain control of New England. After the British victory in 1763, the Treaty of Paris granted control of all land east of the Mississippi to Britain. The bitter and bloody struggle had come to an end.

The Father of New France

Samuel de Champlain (circa 1567–1635) established France's colonial empire in North America. On July 3, 1608, he founded the first permanent settlement, Quebec, in what is now Canada. From Quebec, he set sail to reach the waters of Lake Champlain and discover the land that would become Vermont.

▼ The introduction of muskets changed the balance of power among Native cultures, as shown in this engraving of a battle between Champlain, with his Native American allies, and a rival Native group.

Not Quite a Colony

The Treaty of Paris did not bring peace to Vermont, however. The region was the subject of land disputes between the colonies of New York and New Hampshire, which both claimed ownership.

From 1749 to 1763, the royal governor of New Hampshire, Benning Wentworth, issued 131 land grants in Vermont. These came to be known as the "New Hampshire Grants." In 1764, however, Britain's King George III ruled that New York had jurisdiction over Vermont. Those who had already purchased grants from the New Hampshire governor faced financial ruin because New York also required payment. Numerous land disputes between New York and New Hampshire colonists marked the years leading up to the Revolutionary War.

By 1770, the territorial conflicts led Ethan Allen, a Vermont landowner under a New Hampshire grant, to organize a band of fellow grant holders to resist the "Yorkers." The rugged company of fighters came to be

▼ Early in the Revolutionary War, Ethan Allen captured Fort Ticonderoga on Lake Champlain in New York. Allen and his Green Mountain Boys attacked at dawn on May 10, 1775, waking up the fort's commander.

known as the Green Mountain Boys. The skirmishes subsided only when news of the Revolutionary War reached Vermont. At that point, Allen and his men turned their attention to fighting the British.

The Revolutionary War

Ethan Allen was captured by the British early in the war. The Green Mountain Boys, now under the command of Allen's cousin, Colonel Seth Warner, played a major role in the 1777 battles of Hubbardton and Bennington. The Battle of Bennington was a key event in the war. Named for the Vermont town the British had intended to attack, the battle actually took place in New York.

That same year, Vermont's settlers requested that the Continental Congress recognize the area as the fourteenth state. The request was denied. Vermont then declared itself the independent republic of New Connecticut. The republic adopted a constitution that outlawed slavery and allowed every male — whether a property owner or not — to vote.

Freed in 1778, after over two years in a British jail, a frustrated Ethan Allen tried to guarantee that Vermont would not be swallowed up by New York or New Hampshire, both of which still laid claim to the region. Those states, which had seats in Congress, were able to block Vermont's petitions for statehood. Allen instead negotiated with the governor of Canada to guarantee Vermont its independence as a British dominion. Meanwhile, New Hampshire was particularly unhappy with Vermonters because they had convinced some western New Hampshire towns to join their struggle to become a state.

After the end of the Revolutionary War in 1783, Congress decided to send troops to overthrow the Vermont government, but George Washington intervened. Eventually, New York and New Hampshire were persuaded to give up their rival claims to the region, and Vermont became the fourteenth state in 1791.

Ethan Allen

Ethan Allen's (1738–1789) leadership inspired the devotion of his famed band of fighters, the Green Mountain Boys. George Washington once wrote of Allen, "There is an original something about him that commands attention." As a tactician, however, Allen was not always successful.

Allen decided to follow up his victory at Fort Ticonderoga by invading Canada. The attempt ended with his capture, and he was sent to England to be tried for treason. He spent two years in captivity.

After the war's end, Allen was again at the center of controversy. His resolute championship of Vermont's independence inspired admiration, but his methods eventually led to accusations of treason, this time by the United States. The charges were made because Allen had negotiated with Canada to make Vermont a British province. Allen claimed that the negotiations were pressure tactics designed to force Congress to accept Vermont as a state, although no records survived to prove this. The treason charges were dropped, and Allen died in 1789, two years before Vermont achieved statehood.

The War of 1812

In 1809, the governor-general of Canada hired Vermonter John Henry to find out if the New England states might be persuaded to secede and reunite with Britain. Henry was never paid by the Canadian government for his work, and so, as revenge, sold his correspondence with the governor-general to President James Madison in 1812. Along with other issues, public outrage over the correspondence helped push the United States to declare war on Britain.

The war was unpopular with many New Englanders, who feared that it would ruin their trade with Britain. In fact, throughout the war, New England profited by smuggling goods to the British.

Vermont and New York each shared a border with the British dominion, Canada, and were therefore of strategic importance in the conflict. Ships from the British fleet patrolled within U.S. territory on the waters of Lakes Champlain, George, and Erie.

In 1813, a young U.S. naval officer, Thomas Macdonough, was dispatched to create a fleet of U.S. ships to challenge Britain's naval superiority on Lake Champlain. Macdonough chose the town of Vergennes in western Vermont for a naval yard. Among the battleships built and launched from Vergennes were the *Saratoga* and the

▲ The painting above depicts Thomas Macdonough aboard the *Saratoga* as he commands his men during the 1814 Battle of Plattsburgh. It was painted by U.S. artist Alonzo Chappel around 1860.

DID YOU KNOW?

Vermont women were first allowed to vote in 1820 but only in local district elections.

Ticonderoga. On September 11, 1814, these ships defeated the British navy in the Battle of Plattsburgh. The British negotiated for peace, and the war officially ended with the Treaty of Ghent on December 24, 1814.

Growth and Expansion

In 1823, the Champlain Canal was completed, connecting Lake Champlain to New York's Hudson River. It provided a new trade route for Vermont to ship its goods to the people of New York and beyond. The extension of three major rail lines into Vermont in the mid-1800s further increased the possibilities for the import and export of goods, information, and, of course, people.

The main rail line connecting Boston, Massachusetts, to Montreal in Canada brought immigrants from many European countries to the state. Among these immigrants were skilled Italian and Welsh stoneworkers who found employment in the state's marble and granite quarries. Large numbers of French Canadians arrived, as well as Irish immigrants fleeing the potato famine of the 1840s. All of these people provided labor for the state's railways and mills.

The Civil War

Approximately thirty-five thousand soldiers from Vermont fought in the Civil War. While little action took place in the northeast, Vermont was the site of the northernmost Confederate action against the Union. In 1864, twenty-two Confederate soldiers robbed several banks in St. Albans and fled to Canada with thousands of dollars.

After the war, Vermont's agricultural industry experienced a slump. Many people moved west to new lands with more favorable climates, or to cities to work in factories. Textile mills moved out of the state in search of cheaper labor, but the granite industry still boomed. Meanwhile, the ability to transport goods via railroads in refrigerated cars resulted in an increase in dairy farming. The refrigerated cars enabled dairy farmers to market their products outside the state.

▶ The Champlain Canal, which opened in 1823, provides a water route between New York and Vermont. In this 1939 photograph, pleasure boats pass through the canal's locks.

Freezing Summer

In 1815, a volcano erupted in Indonesia. It sent so much ash into the atmosphere that it affected weather worldwide. Vermont's weather took a drastic turn. May 1816 was cold and dry, but on June 5 temperatures soared to 90° Fahrenheit (32° Celsius). The next day it began to snow, burying parts of Vermont under more than 1 foot (0.3 meters), destroying crops and killing livestock. Vermont's previous growing seasons had also been plagued by bad weather. Convinced that the weather had taken a permanent turn for the worse, many left the state — so many that some towns were completely abandoned.

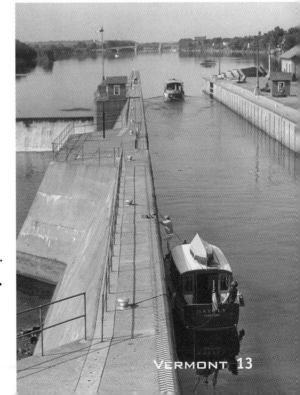

The Twentieth Century

In 1881, as the nineteenth century was drawing to a close, Vermonter Chester A. Arthur rose to the U.S. presidency. Later, in the 1920s, Plymouth Notch native Calvin Coolidge would follow in his footsteps. On the economic front Vermont had become known, by the early twentieth century, for its stone quarries, which produced high-quality marble as well as slate and granite. Manufacturing replaced agriculture as the state's big moneymaker. The production of machine parts and other metal goods soared between 1900 and 1920 as Vermont helped the United States arm for World War I.

A great flood wreaked havoc in Vermont in 1927, and the resulting reconstruction changed the state forever. Rather than repairing the old transportation system of dirt roads and railway lines, the state created a system of paved roads that brought Vermont rolling into the motor age. The cost of all this work resulted in the introduction of a state income tax. It wasn't until the 1950s, however, that the state began building its two interstate highways.

Vermont's tourist industry flourished early in the twentieth century, as vacation camps and resort hotels appeared throughout the region. In 1911, Vermont became the first state to establish a bureau of tourism. The tourism industry could not protect Vermont from the Great Depression that struck the nation in 1929, however. Vermonters struggled financially as factories and lumber mills closed. With the help of government programs, the economy began to bounce back in the late 1930s.

During World War II, many of Vermont's factories were used to produce war materials. The state used those factories to develop new industries after the war ended.

Meanwhile, agriculture continued its slow decline, becoming less and less significant to the state's economy. While there were fewer farms, the ones that remained grew larger. This was made possible, in part, because much of the population moved to urban areas.

From 1860 through 1960, the state's electoral college votes went to the Republican presidential nominee in every election. Then, in 1964, Lyndon Johnson became the first Democratic nominee to win Vermont's electoral votes in a century. Within three decades the Democratic party would come to dominate the state's politics. Vermont is now considered one of the most liberal states in the nation.

A Natural Attraction

During the 1960s and 1970s, Vermont saw a sizable influx of city dwellers relocating to greener pastures as part of the communal, back-to-the-land movement popular in those days. For these people, Vermont was an ideal place to live, with its natural lush surroundings, rural serenity, and history of progressive thought.

In 1984, the state of Vermont designated almost one-quarter of its land as wilderness by establishing six wilderness areas in Green Mountain National Forest. Aware of the potential for tourism and wary of encroaching development, the state government also enacted a series of planning and development controls to stem urban growth.

During the later years of the twentieth century, Vermont continued to utilize its natural resources sensibly and carefully. While small farms still thrive, the state has embraced tourism as an essential part of its economy. The fierce independent spirit of Vermonters is still strong today, thanks to a rich history and a hearty appreciation of the gifts nature has bestowed upon them.

A President's Words

"I love Vermont because of her hills and valleys, her scenery and invigorating climate, but most of all, because of her indomitable people. They are a race of pioneers who have almost beggared themselves to serve others. If the spirit of liberty should vanish in other parts of the union and support of our institutions should languish, it could all be replenished from the generous store held by the people of this brave little state of Vermont."

— *President Calvin Coolidge, from a speech given at Bennington, September 21, 1928*

▼ Barre calls itself the Granite Center of the World. This 1917 photograph shows the railroad that transported granite out of town.

A Spirit of Independence

Thetford Center, Vermont, looks much like any of two or three hundred other small New England villages — except for one thing. It still has a dozen tiny hayfields scattered through it.

— *Noel Perrin*, Last Person Rural, *1991*

With a population of just over 600,000, Vermont is the least populous state east of the Mississippi River. In the West, only Wyoming has fewer residents. U.S. Census figures for the year 2000 indicate that the population grew 8.2 percent between 1990 and 2000. The Census also estimated that there are approximately 66 residents per square mile (25 residents per sq km) in Vermont compared to a national average of about 80 per square mile (31 per sq km). In 2000, the population of Burlington, the state's largest urban center, was just under thirty-nine thousand people, with about one hundred thousand more in the greater metropolitan area. The next largest communities in the state are Essex, Rutland, Colchester, and South Burlington.

More than two-thirds of Vermonters live in rural areas. Maine is the only other New England state that has a

Age Distribution in Vermont
(2000 Census)

0–4	33,989
5–19	132,268
20–24	37,852
25–44	176,456
45–64	150,752
65 & over	77,510

Across One Hundred Years

Vermont's three largest foreign-born groups for 1890 and 1990

Total state population: 332,422
Total foreign-born: 44,088 (13%)

Total state population: 562,758
Total foreign-born: 17,544 (3%)

Patterns of Immigration

The total number of people who immigrated to Vermont in 1998 was 513. Of that number, the largest immigrant groups were from Canada (10.7%), India (10.3%), and China (5.8%).

larger rural than urban population. The people who live in Vermont's almost three hundred small towns and villages take their roles as citizens seriously. Most are active participants in their annual town meetings, which are a form of local government in the state.

The majority of Vermont workers are employed in manufacturing, trade, or service-related industries. The median income for families in Vermont is $59,125. For individuals the figure is $20,308. According to the U.S. Census Bureau, 9.7 percent of Vermonters in the year 2000 lived in poverty. This percentage is lower than the national average.

▲ Burlington, on the edge of Lake Champlain, is the state's largest city.

Ethnicity

As a rural state with a small population, Vermont is among the least racially diverse states in the nation. Whites make up 96.8 percent of the residents, compared to a national average of about 75 percent. African Americans, Hispanics, and Asians each constitute less than 1 percent of the total population, and Native Americans now number

Heritage and Background, Vermont   Year 2000

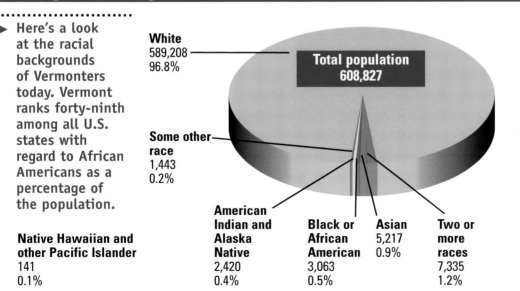

▶ Here's a look at the racial backgrounds of Vermonters today. Vermont ranks forty-ninth among all U.S. states with regard to African Americans as a percentage of the population.

White
589,208
96.8%

Total population
608,827

Some other race
1,443
0.2%

American Indian and Alaska Native
2,420
0.4%

Black or African American
3,063
0.5%

Asian
5,217
0.9%

Two or more races
7,335
1.2%

Native Hawaiian and other Pacific Islander
141
0.1%

Note: 0.9% (5,504) of the population identify themselves as **Hispanic** or **Latino,** a cultural designation that crosses racial lines. Hispanics and Latinos are counted in this category as well as the racial category of their choice.

approximately 2,500. The vast majority of Vermont's current residents were born in the United States. For many years, Canadians have been the state's largest immigrant group. People have also emigrated from Italy, Ireland, and Germany over the years. Recently immigrants from China and India have made homes in Vermont.

Perspectives

The traditional New England "Yankee" traits of thrift, modesty, a strong work ethic, and respect for the individual are typical of Vermonters. From the early days as a republic to modern times, respect for individuals has been expressed in Vermont's laws. Vermont's original constitution, drafted in 1777, made slavery illegal and gave the right to vote to all men at a time when other states required men to be landholders to vote. In recent years, Vermont became the

Educational Levels of Vermont Workers (age 25 and over)

Less than 9th grade	30,945
9th to 12th grade, no diploma	37,692
High school graduate, including equivalency	123,430
Some college, no degree or associate degree	78,324
Bachelor's degree	55,120
Graduate or professional degree	31,734

Setting Priorities

Justin Smith Morrill, both U.S. representative and senator from Vermont, sponsored the nation's first land-grant legislation, which became law in 1862. Under this law, the federal government gave each state 30,000 acres (12,141 ha) of land for each representative and senator to fund colleges that would offer both a practical and traditional education to people who could not otherwise afford higher education. The University of Vermont (already in existence) was among the first grant recipients.

▼ Painter Hall at Middlebury College is the oldest college building in Vermont, dating from 1815.

first state to legally sanction same-sex unions, granting partners many of the same rights as married couples.

Vermonters are primarily Christian. There is a strong Roman Catholic influence, which originated with the French who first held services in 1666 at their shrine to Saint Anne on the Isle La Motte in Lake Champlain. The arrival of settlers from the New England colonies in subsequent years meant that Protestant traditions — including Episcopalian, Methodist, Baptist, and Congregationalist — became dominant. The middle of the nineteenth century brought French Canadian, Irish, and Italian immigrants to Vermont. They brought with them their Roman Catholic faith, which is still the denomination to which most Vermont church members belong.

▲ The Vermont ethic of self-sufficiency comes out in the popular local markets, like this one in Waterbury, where farmers from the area sell their own fresh produce.

Education

Vermont has always taken education seriously. Its first constitution required every town to have a public school. Current law requires that children attend school from the ages of seven through sixteen, and, on average, more money is spent per student in Vermont than the national average. Student–teacher ratios in the state are also lower than the national average. More than 80 percent of Vermonters earn high school diplomas.

Higher education in Vermont not only serves its intended purpose but is also an important source of outside funds and jobs. There are more than twenty private and public colleges and universities in Vermont, in which approximately forty-five thousand students from around the world are enrolled at any given time. The oldest of these is the University of Vermont in Burlington, which was established in 1791. Other prominent colleges and universities in the state include Bennington College, Middlebury College, and the School for International Training in Brattleboro.

Poetry in Vermont

Although born in San Francisco, the famous poet Robert Frost moved to Massachusetts as a boy and spent a significant portion of his adult life in New Hampshire and Vermont. He was named poet laureate of Vermont by the Vermont state legislature in 1961. When Frost died in 1963, his ashes were interred at Old Bennington Cemetery in Bennington.

Rugged Natural Beauty

> Vermont has always taken environmental protection seriously. We were one of the first states to keep billboards off our highways, provide a deposit for bottles, and pass legislation that encourages responsible development.
>
> — *Bernard Sanders, U.S. representative from Vermont, to* The Boston Globe, *2001*

From its granite peaks to the clear waters of its many lakes and rivers, Vermont is a state of breathtaking natural beauty. Formed over the course of several ice ages, the rolling, mountainous landscape is the result of the advance and retreat of glaciers. Each year as winter snows melt into the streams of a new spring, the land stirs to life.

Vermont is located at the westernmost edge of New England. The Connecticut River defines the eastern border, separating the state from New Hampshire. More than half of Vermont's western boundary runs down the middle of Lake Champlain, which also borders New York and the Canadian province of Quebec. Vermont shares its roughly 90-mile (145-km) northern border with Canada. Its short southern border, shared with Massachusetts, is about 40 miles (64 km) long.

Mountains and Valleys

The Green Mountain range, part of the Appalachian Mountain range, defines the Vermont landscape. It consists of two roughly parallel ridges that extend north–south about 250 miles (402 km). The range's Mount Mansfield is

Highest Point

Mt. Mansfield
4,393 feet (1,339 m)
above sea level

▼ Splendid Vermont *(from left to right)*: the shores of Lake Champlain; a wild turkey; a farm in a Vermont valley; Green Mountain scenery dusted white with snow; autumn in Vermont; the Quechee Gorge.

Vermont's highest point. Also within the range is the Long Trail, a long-distance hiking trail that stretches from the Massachusetts border to Canada. The southern portion of this trail coincides with the Appalachian Trail.

In the southwestern part of the state are the Taconic Mountains, which contain valuable marble deposits. The Northeast Highlands are an extension of New Hampshire's White Mountains, a heavily forested range. Their solid core of granite has proved to be one of the state's most important natural resources.

The lowland areas along bodies of water define the state's eastern and western boundaries. In the northwest is the Champlain Valley, an area of rolling hills and fertile land. The region encompasses numerous dairy farms and apple orchards, as well as the state's largest city, Burlington. The Vermont Valley, which lies between the Taconic and the Green Mountains, is a narrow region once used as a thoroughfare for settlers migrating northward. Along the eastern border are Vermont's portion of the Western New England Uplands. The Connecticut River Valley falls within this area. The valley's fertile lowlands gradually rise into the mountain ranges.

Rivers and Lakes

Most of Vermont's eastern rivers and streams run into the Connecticut River, while most of its western rivers flow into Lake Champlain. The more than eight hundred lakes and ponds throughout the state feed the numerous rivers and streams that provide natural irrigation as well as habitats for an abundance of fish. The Connecticut River is a well-traveled waterway used for trade and transportation.

The largest body of water in Vermont is Lake Champlain, although only about 56 percent of the lake is contained within Vermont's boundaries. The remaining

Average January temperature
Burlington: 17°F (-8°C)
Brattleboro: 21°F (-6°C)

Average July temperature
Burlington: 70°F (21°C)
Brattleboro: 70°F (21°C)

Average yearly rainfall
Burlington:
 33 inches (84 cm)
Brattleboro:
 41 inches (104 cm)

Average yearly snowfall
Burlington:
 79 inches (201 cm)
Brattleboro:
 75 inches (191 cm)

Major Rivers

Connecticut River
407 miles (655 km)

Otter Creek
100 miles (161 km)

Winooski River
90 miles (145 km)

Lamoille River
85 miles (137 km)

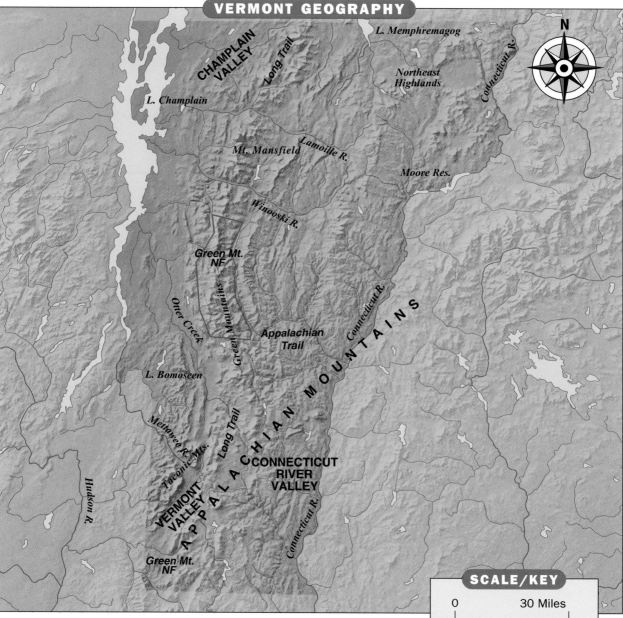

CHAMPLAIN VALLEY

L. Memphremagog

Long Trail

Northeast Highlands

Connecticut R.

L. Champlain

Lamoille R.

Mt. Mansfield

Moore Res.

Winooski R.

Green Mt. NF

Green Mountains

Otter Creek

Appalachian Trail

Connecticut R.

A P P A L A C H I A N   M O U N T A I N S

L. Bomoseen

Long Trail

Mettawee R.

Taconic Mts.

Hudson R.

CONNECTICUT RIVER VALLEY

VERMONT VALLEY

A P P A L A C H I A N

Connecticut R.

Green Mt. NF

area is shared by New York and the province of Quebec in Canada. Lake Bomoseen, which covers an area of approximately 4 square miles (10 sq km), is the largest body of water entirely within Vermont's borders. The lake with the highest elevation in the state is the aptly named Lake of the Clouds, which is nestled on the slopes of Mt. Mansfield at an altitude of approximately 4,000 feet (1,219 m).

The Climate

Vermont has long, frosty winters and beautiful — but short — summers. With hundreds of mountain peaks that rise

DID YOU KNOW?

Vermont is the only New England state that has no seacoast.

thousands of feet above sea level, subzero temperatures are not unheard of at higher elevations in the midst of winter, and the mountains' snowcaps can last year-round. Even during summer, evenings are often cool and crisp.

As winter ends, melting snow results in what many call the Mud Season. Back roads and trails turn to mud, and streams and rivers are subject to flooding. Mud Season gives way to Black Fly Season, which lasts from mid-May through June. Black flies, which bite humans, are at their most numerous during this period.

Plants and Animals

Vermont's land is more than three-fourths forest. The variety of trees within these forests include maple, hickory, oak, butternut, elm, and birch. Pine and other evergreen trees grow mainly in the mountainous regions. Among the smaller plants common in Vermont are many types of ferns as well as wildflowers such as violets, daisies, and anemones.

Moose, bears, bobcats, and deer are among the larger animals in Vermont. Smaller animals such as beavers, foxes, mink, and porcupines are hunted for their fur. Schools of salmon, trout, and bass dart through the rivers, lakes, and streams, while Canada geese, wild turkeys, ducks, and other birds are among the array of wildlife common to the state.

Largest Lakes
Lake Champlain 278,400 acres (112,668 ha)
Lake Memphremagog 19,200 acres (7,770 ha)
Lake Bomoseen 2,360 acres (955 ha)

▼ The spectacular fall foliage of Vermont's forests attracts visitors to the state. Waits River (*below*), a classic New England village in eastern Vermont, comes alive with color.

Making a Living in Vermont

> To make . . . and sell the finest quality all natural ice cream and related products in . . . innovative flavors made from Vermont dairy products.
>
> — from the mission statement of Ben & Jerry's Homemade, Inc.

Early Vermont settlers worked the land, cultivating just enough to satisfy the immediate needs of their communities. Then improved roads and shipping routes made it possible to trade with other communities in New England and Canada. Wood products, potatoes, grain, and livestock were among Vermont's early exports.

In the early 1800s farmers raised merino sheep for wool, but competition from the West led many to turn to dairy farming. Like other parts of New England in the mid-1800s, Vermont's economy also moved toward manufacturing. Today, manufacturing and farming are still significant to the state's economy, but since the early 1900s tourism has become increasingly important.

Agriculture

Farmland covers almost one-fourth of Vermont's land area. Of the more than six thousand working farms in the state today, many are of the smaller variety that provide goods at farmer's markets or roadside vegetable stands. Commonly cultivated crops include apples, potatoes, sweet corn, garden vegetables, and honey. Lumber, Christmas trees, and greenhouse nursery products are also profitable products for local vendors.

Dairy farming has been the main agricultural activity in the state ever since the invention of refrigerated rail cars in 1851. Vermont produces approximately 2 billion pounds (908 million kg) of milk each year. Nearly half of all the milk consumed in New England comes from Vermont. Cheese, ice cream, butter, yogurt, and eggs are also produced and are

Top Employers (of workers age sixteen and over)
Services 35.1%
Wholesale and retail trade 22.0%
Manufacturing . . 15.5%
Construction 7.8%
Finance, insurance, and real estate 5.6%
Transportation, communications, and other public utilities 5.2%
Public Administration . . . 4.3%
Agriculture, forestry, and fisheries 4.2%
Mining 0.3%

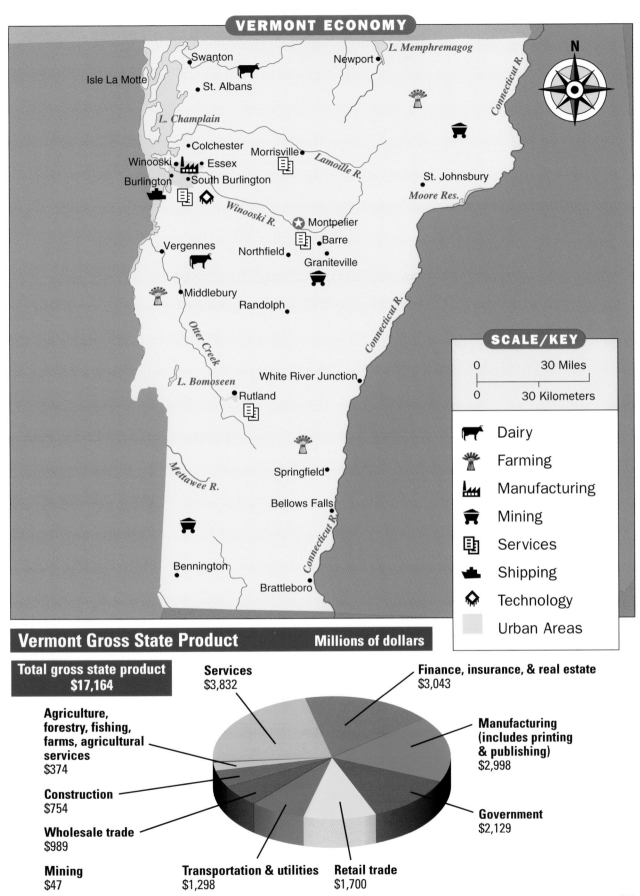

VERMONT ECONOMY

L. Memphremagog
Swanton
Newport
Isle La Motte
St. Albans
L. Champlain
Colchester
Morrisville
Lamoille R.
Winooski
Essex
St. Johnsbury
Burlington
South Burlington
Moore Res.
Winooski R.
Montpelier
Vergennes
Barre
Northfield
Graniteville
Middlebury
Randolph
Otter Creek
L. Bomoseen
White River Junction
Rutland
Mettawee R.
Springfield
Bellows Falls
Bennington
Brattleboro
Connecticut R.

SCALE/KEY

0	30 Miles
0	30 Kilometers

- Dairy
- Farming
- Manufacturing
- Mining
- Services
- Shipping
- Technology
- Urban Areas

Vermont Gross State Product — Millions of dollars

Total gross state product $17,164

- Services $3,832
- Finance, insurance, & real estate $3,043
- Manufacturing (includes printing & publishing) $2,998
- Agriculture, forestry, fishing, farms, agricultural services $374
- Construction $754
- Wholesale trade $989
- Mining $47
- Transportation & utilities $1,298
- Retail trade $1,700
- Government $2,129

exported far and wide. Vermont leads the New England states in the production of milk, hay, and dairy cattle and leads the nation in maple syrup production.

Manufacturing

Nearly one-third of the income generated in Vermont by industrial activity in the 1990s came from the production of electrical equipment and electronic components. Large corporations such as IBM, which is the single largest corporate employer in the state, have operations in Vermont. These companies produce computer components, semiconductors, and other machinery parts and supplies. Although only about 15 percent of the state's workers are employed in areas of manufacturing, the products they produce affect the livelihood of the Vermonters who work in wholesale and retail jobs.

Printing and publishing play an important role in Vermont's economy. Books, business forms, and newspapers are the leading products. The state's other manufacturing firms produce aircraft engines and parts, wood furniture, and metalworking machinery.

Granite, a very hard rock used in buildings, is the leading mined product. Large amounts of slate, talc, limestone, gravel, and sand are also mined for export. The western part of the state is known for its fine marble, which has been used to create several U.S. landmarks, including the Jefferson Memorial and the U.S. Supreme Court building.

Tourism

Roughly 35 percent of Vermont's labor force works in service-related fields. Many of these workers have jobs that are directly related to the state's tourism industry — for example, travel agents as well as hotel, restaurant, and ski resort employees.

Sweet Sap

Long before European settlers arrived, the Abenaki were making maple syrup. The sap of the sugar maple tree is thin and colorless and contains only about 3 percent sugar. It runs naturally from the tree from the first spring thaw to the time when the tree's buds turn to leaves. The distinctive taste comes about during a boiling process — it takes 40 gallons (151 liters) of sap to produce 1 gallon (4 l) of syrup.

▼ Vermont slate is used in building projects throughout the world.

Major Airport		
Airport	Location	Passengers per year (2001)
Burlington International	Burlington	1,035,238

Made in Vermont

Leading farm products and crops
Milk
Apples
Maple syrup
Eggs
Cheese
Honey
Nursery plants
Vegetables
Small fruits
Christmas trees
Lumber
Livestock (cattle, sheep, pigs, chickens)

Other products
Granite
Electronic parts
Machine tools
Furniture
Books
Computer components
Specialty foods

Shopkeepers, hairdressers, and real estate agents benefit from increased tourism. Other service industries include private medical care, insurance, and financial services.

Skiing is the single most important tourist industry in the state and an excellent example of how the state's industries are related. Developing ski resorts requires builders, and so the construction industry benefits. As skiers fill the hotels and restaurants, roads are improved to accommodate the increased traffic. More jobs and improved transit attract new residents who provide labor for local manufacturers, and thus the entire economy is stimulated.

Trade and Transportation

Vermont has a great deal of trade interaction with its northern neighbor, Canada. St. Albans, near Lake Champlain, is the port of entry for rail freight coming from Canada. Five different rail lines offer freight service in Vermont. Major rail imports include lumber and animal feed. Burlington, which lies on the shore of Lake Champlain, is the state's primary port of entry for goods shipped from Canada or for freight arriving by way of the Hudson River. A large amount of the state's fuel oil arrives by tanker at Burlington.

Power

Nearly 80 percent of Vermont's electricity is generated by one nuclear power plant — the Vermont Yankee — located in the southeastern town of Vernon. Run by a company of the same name, the 550-megawatt facility was first opened in 1972. Hydroelectric facilities provide up to 19 percent of the state's energy; wood-fueled plants generate the remainder.

▶ Marble used to build the Supreme Court building in Washington, D.C., came from Vermont quarries.

Independent Minds

> Ever since I arrived to a state of manhood, and acquainted myself with the history of mankind, I have felt a sincere passion for liberty.
>
> — *Ethan Allen,* A Narrative of Colonel Ethan Allen's Captivity, *1779*

From the beginning Vermont has displayed a political independence and an openness to change. Its original 1777 constitution, in which Vermont declared itself an independent republic, was the most liberal of its day, giving all adult male citizens the right to vote regardless of race, religion, or land ownership. It also outlawed slavery — the first constitution to do so. A second constitution guaranteeing the same rights was adopted in 1786 before Vermont officially became the fourteenth state on March 4, 1791. Finally, in 1793 it adopted its current constitution.

Vermonters can propose amendments, or changes, to the state constitution every four years. The Vermont Senate must approve the proposed amendment by a two-thirds vote and the House of Representatives by a simple majority vote. Then, at the next legislative session, proposals must receive a majority vote by both the house and senate before being put before the voters. Finally, a majority of the popular vote is required for an amendment to become law. This process often takes five years.

Executive Branch

The chief executive of Vermont is the governor, who is elected to a two-year term and can serve an unlimited number of terms. He or she is responsible for proposing the state budget and also appoints approximately three hundred state officials. Many of the appointments require senate approval. In addition to the governor, voters also elect the lieutenant governor, attorney general, secretary of state, treasurer, and auditor of accounts to two-year terms.

State Constitution

That all persons are born equally free and independent, and have certain natural, inherent, and unalienable rights, amongst which are enjoying and defending life and liberty, acquiring, possessing and protecting property, and pursuing and obtaining happiness and safety; therefore no person born in this country, or brought from over sea, ought to be holden by law, to serve any person as a servant, slave or apprentice, after arriving to the age of twenty-one years, unless bound by the person's own consent, after arriving to such age, or bound by law for the payment of debts, damages, fines, costs, or the like.

— *from the Vermont Constitution, adopted in 1793*

Elected Posts in the Executive Branch		
Office	Length of Term	Term Limits
Governor	2 years	None
Lieutenant Governor	2 years	None
Treasurer	2 years	None
Secretary of State	2 years	None
Auditor of Accounts	2 years	None
Attorney General	2 years	None

Legislative Branch

The state legislature of Vermont is known as the General Assembly. It has two houses — a 150-member house of representatives and a thirty-member senate. All members of the General Assembly serve two-year terms. Legislative sessions are held every year, usually beginning on the first Wednesday after the first Monday in January. The governor may call special sessions if he or she chooses.

Judicial Branch

Vermont's highest court, the supreme court, has a chief justice and four associate justices. The governor nominates the justices to six-year terms, subject to approval by the legislature. Most of the cases the supreme court hears are appeals of decisions made by lower courts.

▼ The state capitol in Montpelier, shown below, was completed in 1859. It is built of granite from Barre.

The other important state courts are the superior courts and the district courts. The superior courts hear civil suits — disputes that are not criminal. There are twelve superior court judges whom the governor nominates to six-year terms with legislative approval. Criminal cases are usually heard in the district courts, where judges are also appointed to six-year terms. County courts, probate courts, and other local courts have judges who are elected to two-year terms.

Local Government

Since colonial days, the major business of town government has been open to the participation of all citizens. Town meetings are held annually on the first Tuesday in March. At these meetings, officials are elected, municipal budgets are approved, school proposals are passed, and many other local issues are voted on from the floor, as they have been for the past two hundred years. Any change proposed to a town charter must be submitted to the Vermont General Assembly for approval.

Political Shifts

Although the state has shifted its party affiliation in recent decades, Vermont was once a staunchly Republican state. No other state has voted for more Republican presidential candidates. No Democrat from Vermont was elected to the U.S. House of Representatives before 1958, when William Meyer won a seat. From 1854 to 1963, all of Vermont's governors were Republican, and it wasn't until 1974 that Patrick J. Leahy became the first Vermont Democrat since the early 1800s to be elected to the U.S. Senate.

Today, Vermont is predominantly Democratic and fairly liberal in its outlook. Vermonters, however, have not settled for being limited to just two parties. In addition to the two major political parties, many other parties play a part in Vermont politics, including the Constitution Party of Vermont, the Vermont Grassroots Party, the Progressive Party of Vermont, and the Socialist Party of Vermont.

General Assembly			
House	**Number of Members**	**Length of Term**	**Term Limits**
Senate	30 senators	2 years	None
House of Representatives	150 representatives	2 years	None

The White House via Vermont

CHESTER ALAN ARTHUR (1881–1885)

Chester Alan Arthur was born on October 5, 1829, in Fairfield, Vermont. Arthur graduated from Union College and taught school before becoming a lawyer. He was a member of the Republican party, which was formed, in part, to oppose slavery. As an abolitionist, Arthur sometimes put his legal skills to use defending runaway slaves. Arthur was elected vice president under President James A. Garfield in 1880. He was sworn in as the nation's twenty-first president on September 20, 1881, following Garfield's assassination, eight months after he took office.

JOHN CALVIN COOLIDGE (1923–1929)

Born on July 4, 1872, in Plymouth Notch, Vermont, John Calvin Coolidge became the nation's thirtieth president on August 3, 1923. Coolidge graduated from Amherst College and practiced law before venturing into politics. His political career began in Northampton, Massachusetts, where he was elected city councilman in 1899. Eventually, he became governor of the state. In 1921, he was sworn in as vice president under Warren G. Harding and succeeded to the presidency in 1923 when Harding died. He was elected to the presidency in 1924. Coolidge was considered to be an effective leader; he believed that "the business of America is business." At the end of his term, he retired to private life.

On the national level, Vermont has only three electoral votes, and it elects two senators and one representative. Vermont's representative in the House is known as a "representative at large" because he or she is not from a specific district. As of the year 2002, one senator was a Democrat and both of the other positions were filled by Independents.

▶ In 2001, U.S. senator James Jeffords of Vermont left the Republican party and became an Independent. The result of the switch was the elimination of the slim Republican majority in the Senate.

Four Seasons of Life

> There is no dignity quite so impressive, and no independence quite so important, as living within your means.
> — *President Calvin Coolidge*

Postcard images of white clapboard houses, covered bridges, and a herd of cows grazing next to an old tractor paint a charming — and quite accurate — picture of Vermont. Although there are urban areas and bustling resorts, the majority of Vermont's people live in rural towns where life moves at a leisurely pace.

An Artistic Inspiration

Vermont's pastoral landscapes and beautiful vistas have long attracted writers, painters, poets, and musicians searching for artistic inspiration. Grandma Moses, who began her painting career when she was seventy-five, and Norman Rockwell, who was one of the most famous U.S. illustrators, both painted warm scenes of small-town life inspired by Vermont's rural communities. Novelist John Irving, like poet Robert Frost before him, has taken inspiration from the ruggedness of the Vermont spirit as well as from its natural beauty.

Other famous authors who have lived in Vermont include Sinclair Lewis and Shirley Jackson. Karen Hesse and Katherine Paterson, Newbery Award-winning children's authors, live and write in Vermont today. Meanwhile, the Bread Loaf Writers Conference at Middlebury College attracts

Big Bessie

The Holstein cow, known for its large black and white spots, is the most common breed of cow in Vermont and produces more milk than any other breed. The average Holstein weighs about 1,500 pounds (680 kg) and can produce about 6 gallons (23 l) of milk per day.

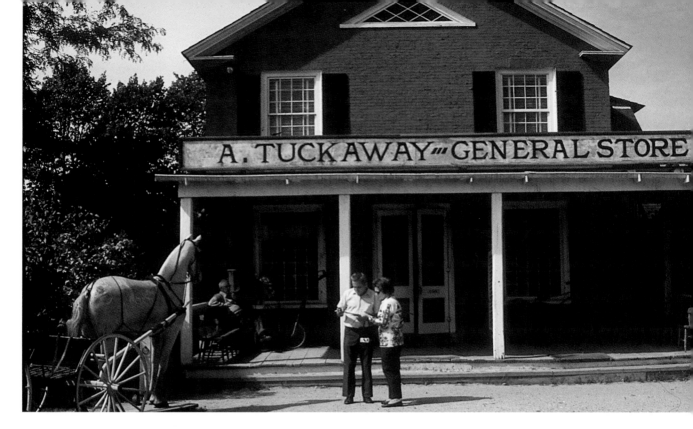

faculty and students from all over the nation. It is the oldest U.S. writers' conference.

Vermont is also home to hundreds of art galleries and regional theaters where local talent is proudly displayed. In every corner of Vermont, local traditions such as quilting and woodworking combine with the work of novelists, the modern canvases of local painters, and music played by classically trained musicians to create a rich tapestry of cultural life.

▲ The A. Tuckaway General Store is part of the Shelburne Museum, which houses the largest collection of Americana in the United States.

Museums and More

Many of the state's museums highlight Vermont's traditional heritage. The Shelburne Museum's displays include whole buildings, most moved there from various locations around New England. This re-creation of an old New England village consists of about thirty-five buildings that give visitors a glimpse of life in another time.

Each summer, world-famous music festivals such as the Discover Jazz Festival and the Marlboro Music Festival draw thousands to outdoor concerts. Since the 1930s, the Vermont Symphony Orchestra has been thrilling audiences with as many as fifty concerts per year.

In St. Johnsbury, visitors can tour the world's largest maple candy factory and sample some of the products. The Bread and Puppet Museum in Glover is home to the world's

Real Vermont

"I like Vermont because it is quiet, because you have a population that is solid and not driven mad by the American mania — that mania which considers a town of 4,000 twice as good as a town of 2,000."

—*Sinclair Lewis, Nobel Prize-winning author and onetime Vermont resident*

largest collection of giant puppets. These puppets have been used for more than twenty-five years in performances of the Bread and Puppet Circus, a political theater group that continues to perform in demonstrations throughout the country. For fishing enthusiasts, the American Museum of Fly Fishing in Manchester is a must-see. Here visitors can ogle tackle owned by such famous fishermen as Ernest Hemingway, Bing Crosby, and Daniel Webster.

Other museums dedicated to Vermont history include the Ethan Allen Homestead in Burlington; the Brattleboro Museum and Art Center, housed in an old railway station; and the Old Stone House Museum in Brownington.

Big City, Small Capital

There are more than twenty colleges and universities scattered throughout Vermont. The lively collegiate atmosphere is especially strong in the city of Burlington, where a large portion of the city's population consists of students, professors, and other employees of the University of Vermont. The university is one of the oldest in the nation, and its elegant and stately brick buildings, surrounded by greenery, offer a visual reminder of New England's educational traditions.

Burlington is the commercial and industrial center of the state. There are many beautiful old houses, charming

▲ The Green Mountains include the state's highest point and the Long Trail. In 1964, nearly 60,000 acres (24,300 ha) of this region's parkland were officially designated wilderness areas.

DID YOU KNOW?

There are no billboards in the state of Vermont. They have been illegal since the 1960s. Very strict ordinances are in place that allow discreet signs at major intersections but do not allow billboards to be constructed.

shops, a variety of restaurants, and historical landmarks. Although it is small, it bustles with life.

Montpelier has the smallest population of any state capital. One benefit of its small size is that it is an extremely clean and green city. The grand, gold-domed state capitol building, the Vermont State House, is Montpelier's centerpiece.

Smart Choices

Vermonters recognize that nature exists in a delicate balance and must be cared for and maintained. The Green Mountain National Forest, which is divided into northern and southern sectors, covers approximately 350,000 acres (141,645 ha) of land. Even today large sections of the forest remain completely undeveloped, with no electricity, roads, or signage.

With its unspoiled wilderness, rolling hills, and numerous lakes, the Green Mountain Forest offers opportunities for hiking, camping, fishing, and other outdoor pastimes. There are 512 miles (824 km) of trails available for visitors to explore.

Winter

Many of Vermont's quaint towns are transformed into snowy tourist destinations during the winter months. Skiers and snowboarders come from afar to enjoy some of the best resorts in the eastern United States. One-third of all Vermont's tourism income is earned during the ski season. Skiers spend $750 million each year on lift tickets, ski rentals, food, lodging, and other tourist-related expenses.

The largest ski area is Killington, with more than two hundred Alpine skiing and snowboarding runs, hundreds of condos and vacation homes, and spectacular ski lodges. The entire region centers on

▼ Visitors flock to Vermont in winter to enjoy such activities as snowmobiling *(inset)* and skiing *(bottom)*.

tourism. Due to its high
elevation, the ski season
there can last up to eight
months of the year.

Winter sports enthusiasts
have enjoyed Stowe since the
1930s. The town looks like
an Alpine village and boasts
some of Vermont's best
slopes. A variety of spas and
resorts offer year-round relaxation. From Stowe
Village, Mountain Road leads to the state's highest
peak, Mount Mansfield.

Sugarbush and Mount Snow also draw many skiers each
year along with dozens of other towns and resorts. Downhill
skiing and snowboarding, however, are not the only games
in town during winter. The state's hundreds of frozen lakes
and ponds provide opportunities for skating, hockey, and ice
fishing, while the snow-covered hills are great for cross-
country skiing, snowshoeing, and snowmobiling.

Vermonters put their state's ski slopes to good use. After
the 2002 Winter Olympics, two Vermonters brought home
a gold medal each. Kelly Clark won the women's snowboard
halfpipe event, and Ross Powers won the men's.

▲ Bicyclists enjoy the
country scenery on
a Montpelier road.
(*top*). The von Trapp
family, famous as
the family in *The
Sound of Music*,
opened this lodge
in Stowe after they
escaped from Nazi-
controlled Austria
prior to World
War II (*inset*).

The Warm Seasons

After a long, cold winter, the snow melts into the lakes and streams, and Vermonters embrace a whole new set of recreational activities. Swimming and boating are hugely popular, especially along the shores of Lake Champlain and among the numerous islands that are sprinkled throughout its waters. Canoes and kayaks can be seen gliding along the waters, and anglers go fishing for salmon, trout, and bass.

The craggy mountains and rolling hills offer ample opportunities for hiking and rock climbing, while the state parks and forests are popular spots for camping, biking, and water sports.

Autumn

As summer descends into autumn, one of nature's most spectacular shows gets under way. The changing colors of the leaves in Vermont transform the already beautiful landscape into an amazing display of vivid reds, dazzling golds, and blazing oranges. Apples and pumpkins are sold along the roadsides as thousands of visitors drive through the countryside to take in the sights and smells of the season.

Leafing, as this pursuit of brilliant fall foliage is called, is in fact so popular in Vermont that regular reports appear in local newspapers and on the Internet, advising potential leafers on when and where "peak" color will occur. Generally, mid-October is considered prime viewing, but if cool weather arrives early, the color change will happen sooner. Tourists come from all over the world to enjoy this critical period, which lasts only a matter of days.

Just as one fall succeeds another, Vermonters continue going to town meetings, buying local produce and maintaining the relaxed yet traditional lifestyle for which they are famous — protecting the past while looking squarely to the future.

▲ Covered bridges provide part of the charm of Vermont's countryside. The Dummerston bridge (*above*) is the longest covered bridge still in use and open to traffic in the state. It was built in 1872.

Monsters of the Deep

According to local legend, Lake Champlain is home to the Champlain Monster, or the "Champ," a water serpent not unlike the famed Loch Ness Monster. Even Samuel de Champlain wrote of seeing one:

"Many kinds of fish are in great abundance; among others, one the local savages call *chaousarou*. I saw one five feet long, thigh-thick, its head as big as two fists, a beak two and a half feet long, with a double row of sharp, dangerous teeth."

— *Samuel de Champlain*, On the Warpath, *1609*

Patriots to Politicians

Vermont's a place where barns come painted
Red as a strong man's heart
Where stout carts and stout boys in freckles
Are highest forms of art.

— *Robert Tristram Coffin, "Vermont Looks Like a Man,"*
New York Herald Tribune, *January 20, 1955*

Following are only a few of the thousands of people who were born, died, or spent much of their lives in Vermont and made extraordinary contributions to the state and the nation.

LEMUEL HAYNES
PASTOR

BORN: *July 18, 1753, West Hartford, CT*
DIED: *September 18, 1833, Granville, NY*

Born to an African-American father and a white mother, Lemuel Haynes was abandoned by both parents as an infant. At the age of five months, he was indentured to a devout Christian family until he reached twenty-one. The family educated him, encouraging him to study the Bible and the writings of the religious thinkers of the day. In 1775, Haynes joined the revolutionary cause and became one of Paul Revere's Minutemen. His experiences inspired him to write both poetry and an essay, "Liberty Further Extended," that stated, "Liberty is as equally precious to a black man as it is to a white one, and bondage equally intolerable to one as it is to the other." After the war's end, Haynes was ordained as a Congregationalist minister. In 1783, he became the pastor of Rutland, Vermont's West Parish, making him the first African-American minister to a white congregation. He preached more than five thousand sermons over the next thirty years. He was also in wide demand as a speaker and preacher throughout New England and New York. In 1818, he left Rutland to become the pastor in Granville, New York, where he died at the age of eighty.

THOMAS DAVENPORT
INVENTOR

BORN: *July 9, 1802, Williamstown*
DIED: *July 6, 1851, Salisbury*

Thomas Davenport *(left)* was working as a blacksmith in Forestdale when he visited an ironworks in New York in 1833. It was there that he saw a battery-powered electromagnet used to remove iron ore from the surrounding rock. Intrigued by the magnet, he and an associate named Orange Smalley began experimenting with electromagnets. Within about three years, they had used an electromagnet to build a battery-powered electric motor, which Davenport later used to power a printing press. On February 25, 1837, he was issued the first U.S. patent for an electric motor.

JOHN DEERE
ENTREPRENEUR
BORN: *February 7, 1804, Rutland*
DIED: *May 17, 1886, Moline, IL*

After a four-year apprenticeship, John Deere began a career as a blacksmith in 1825. The hayforks, shovels, and other equipment he made were highly prized throughout western Vermont. By the mid-1830s, however, Vermont's economic prospects were bleak, and Deere moved west to a town in Illinois that was home to other former Vermonters. There he found plenty of work and a problem to solve. The iron plows that settlers had brought with them from the east broke when they tried to plow the sod. In 1837, Deere invented the self-scouring steel plow, which cut through the sod. His success led him to found what is now the largest farm machinery company in the world. The company, formed in Moline, Illinois, in 1868, was named Deere & Co. It is said that Deere chose the company's trademark color green for his machines and tools to remind him of his home state.

STEPHEN A. DOUGLAS
POLITICIAN
BORN: *April 23, 1813, Brandon*
DIED: *June 3, 1861, Chicago, IL*

Stephen Arnold Douglas lived in Vermont for his first twenty years, then moved to Illinois. Nicknamed the "Little Giant," he began his political career as attorney general of Illinois in 1834, eventually holding other state offices before being elected to the U.S. House of Representatives in 1843 and to the U.S. Senate in 1847. He ran against Abraham Lincoln for the Illinois Senate seat in 1858 and for the presidency in 1860. Douglas believed that individual territories should decide for themselves whether or not to permit slavery. His debates with Lincoln in 1858 brought Douglas his greatest fame.

WILLIAM MORRIS HUNT
PAINTER
BORN: *March 31, 1824, Brattleboro*
DIED: *September 8, 1879, Isle of Shoals, NH*

After studying art in Paris, William Morris Hunt returned to the United States and established himself in Boston during the 1850s. His

interpretation of the ideals and methods of the French Barbizon school had a great influence on U.S. painting. Hunt eventually opened his own art school and is believed to have been the first U.S. art teacher to accept women into his classes. His painting, *Girl with a Cat,* is shown at left.

ADMIRAL GEORGE DEWEY
COMMANDER OF THE U.S. NAVY

BORN: *December 26, 1837, Montpelier*
DIED: *January 16, 1917, Washington, D.C.*

George Dewey graduated from the U.S. Naval Academy at Annapolis in 1858. He served with Admiral David Farragut in the Battle of New Orleans during the Civil War. In 1897, Dewey was assigned to the U.S. Asiatic Squadron. He came to believe that war with Spain was likely and carefully studied Spain's fleet in the Spanish-held Philippines. In 1898, after the sinking of the U.S. battleship *Maine*, war did break out. Dewey destroyed the Spanish fleet in Manila Bay in the Philippines, without losing the life of a single U.S. sailor. He became a national hero and, in 1899, was appointed admiral of the U.S. Navy. He briefly put himself forward as a presidential candidate in 1900 but then withdrew. Dewey served in the Navy until his death.

WILSON A. BENTLEY
SCIENTIST

BORN: *February 9, 1865, Jericho*
DIED: *December 23, 1931, Jericho*

Wilson Alwyn Bentley was taught at home by his mother until age fourteen. Fascinated by what he saw through a microscope she gave him, he was inspired to photograph snowflakes. After disappointing failures, he finally succeeded and eventually cataloged thousands of snowflakes.

Bentley's interest went beyond the beauty and individuality of each flake — his pictures inspired him to study how both snowflakes and raindrops formed. His theories on weather were published in acclaimed science magazines such as Appleton's *Popular Scientific Monthly*, the *Monthly Weather Review*, and *National Geographic*. In 1924, the first American Meteorological Society research grant was awarded to Bentley for his forty years of work. A volume of his photographs, called *Snow Crystals*, was published in 1931.

ANDREW ELLICOTT DOUGLASS
SCIENTIST

BORN: *July 5, 1867, Windsor*
DIED: *March 20, 1962, Tucson, AZ*

Andrew Ellicott Douglass was a scientist who discovered dendrochronology, or the tree-ring dating method. He found that the age of a tree, as well as the history of the land surrounding it, can be determined by counting and examining the rings inside a tree's trunk. He determined that most trees produce one tree ring (or layer of wood cells) per year and that the rings are wider during moist years and thinner during dry years. Douglass was a professor of astronomy, then dendrochronology, at the University of Arizona. He was also the first person to photograph zodiacal light, or sunlight reflected off meteoroids.

NORMAN ROCKWELL

BORN: *February 3, 1894, New York, NY*
DIED: *November 8, 1978, Stockbridge, MA*

Although born in New York City, Norman Rockwell lived in Arlington during the height of his career, from 1939 to 1953. He gained fame for paintings and illustrations that depicted wholesome small-town life in America. His work graced the covers of many publications, including *The Saturday Evening Post, Ladies' Home Journal,* and *Boys' Life*. Today, in Rutland Town, the Norman Rockwell Museum of Vermont houses a collection that includes more than 2,500 magazine covers, calendars, and advertisements featuring his work.

BOB KEESHAN

CAPTAIN KANGAROO

BORN: *June 27, 1927, Lynbrook, NY*

Robert James Keeshan first became known to TV audiences as Clarabell the Clown on the *Howdy Doody Show* in the early 1950s. He went on to greater fame as Captain Kangaroo on his innovative children's television show of the same name. The show ran for thirty years, first on CBS and then on PBS. Now retired, he lives in Norwich and is a spokesman for the Vermont Children's Trust Foundation.

JERRY GREENFIELD

BORN: *March 14, 1951, Brooklyn, NY*

BEN COHEN

BORN: *March 18, 1951, Brooklyn, NY*

ICE CREAM MOGULS

In 1978, two childhood friends from Merrick, New York, completed a

$5 course in ice-cream making and moved to Vermont. With only $12,000, they opened an ice-cream shop in a converted gas station in Burlington. Using local ingredients, they made ice cream in unusual flavors with quirky names. Word spread about the delicious ice cream, and soon Ben & Jerry's was expanding, selling to stores and restaurants all over the country. In 2000, the company was sold to Unilever for $326 million, but it retains an independent board of directors. Ben and Jerry are famous not only as successful businessmen but also for their philosophy of corporate and social responsibility.

PATTY SHEEHAN

GOLFER

BORN: *October 27, 1956, Middlebury*

Patty Sheehan first joined the Ladies Professional Golf Association (LPGA) in 1980. She won LPGA championships in 1983, 1984, and 1993 and the U.S. Open in both 1992 and 1994. In 1993, she became the youngest golfer ever inducted into the LPGA Hall of Fame. Sheehan is now an editor for a women's golfing magazine in addition to being an active golfer.

Vermont
History At-A-Glance

1609
Samuel de Champlain sets foot in Vermont.

1666
The first permanent European settlement is built on the Isle La Motte in Lake Champlain.

1724
The first permanent English-speaking settlement is established at Fort Dummer.

1749
Governor Benning Wentworth of New Hampshire begins to grant tracts of land to settlers.

1763
The Treaty of Paris grants Great Britain rights to the area of Vermont.

1764
King George III rules that New York, not New Hampshire, has jurisdiction over Vermont.

1770
Ethan Allen organizes the Green Mountain Boys.

1777
The Battles of Hubbardton and Bennington take place; Vermont declares itself an independent republic.

1786
Vermont's second constitution is adopted.

1791
Vermont becomes the fourteenth U.S. state; the University of Vermont is established at Burlington.

1814
Vermont ships play a decisive role in defeating the British at the Battle of Plattsburgh.

1864
Confederate soldiers rob several banks in St. Albans, then flee to Canada.

1600 · **1700** · **1800**

1492
Christopher Columbus comes to New World.

1607
Capt. John Smith and three ships land on Virginia coast and start first English settlement in New World — Jamestown.

1754–63
French and Indian War.

1773
Boston Tea Party.

1776
Declaration of Independence adopted July 4.

1777
Articles of Confederation adopted by Continental Congress.

1787
U.S. Constitution written.

1812–14
War of 1812.

United States
History At-A-Glance

1881
Chester Alan Arthur becomes the twenty-first U.S. president.

1911
Vermont establishes first bureau of tourism in the nation.

1918
Vermont women are given the right to vote in municipal elections.

1923
Calvin Coolidge becomes the thirtieth U.S. president.

1927
A devastating flood hits Vermont.

1954
Vermont's Consuelo N. Bailey is the first woman in the nation to be elected lieutenant governor.

1958
For the first time Vermont elects a Democrat, William Meyer, to serve in the U.S. House of Representatives.

1961
Robert Frost is named poet laureate of Vermont.

1972
Vermont's only nuclear power plant opens.

1974
Patrick J. Leahy is the first Democrat elected to the U.S. Senate since the early 1800s.

1984
Sections of Green Mountain National Forest are set aside by Congress as wilderness areas.

1999
The Vermont Supreme Court mandates that same-sex couples be granted rights and protections of marriage.

1800 — **1900** — **2000**

1848
Gold discovered in California draws eighty thousand prospectors in the 1849 Gold Rush.

1861–65
Civil War.

1869
Transcontinental railroad completed.

1917–18
U.S. involvement in World War I.

1929
Stock market crash ushers in Great Depression.

1941–45
U.S. involvement in World War II.

1950–53
U.S. fights in the Korean War.

1964–73
U.S. involvement in Vietnam War.

2000
George W. Bush wins the closest presidential election in history.

2001
A terrorist attack in which four hijacked airliners crash into New York City's World Trade Center, the Pentagon, and farmland in western Pennsylvania leaves thousands dead or injured.

▼ **In 1927 the town of Springfield turned out to see aviator Charles A. Lindbergh.**

Festivals and Fun for All

Check web site for exact date and directions.

Ben & Jerry's One World One Heart Festival, Warren

A festival for all ages to welcome the long, hot summer with ice-cold ice cream as well as entertainment, music, and fun activities.
www.benjerry.com

Burlington Discover Jazz Festival, Burlington

A six-day celebration of jazz, blues, Latin, and world-beat music with performances by world-class artists.
www.discoverjazz.com

Lake Champlain Balloon and Craft Festival, Vergennes

A magical, three-day festival during which the skies are filled with colorful hot-air balloons.
www.ballooning.net/lcbcf.htm

Marlboro Music Festival, Marlboro

A series of chamber music concerts at Marlboro College are performed by talented young musicians playing side by side with master concert artists.
www.marlboro music.org

Stowe Winter Carnival, Stowe

A carnival of winter sports competitions, entertainment, and wintertime traditions. The first winter carnival was held in 1921.
www.stowewintercarnival.com

Vermont Apple Festival, Springfield

Held in Springfield on Columbus Day weekend, the festival includes live entertainment, apple pie contests, arts and crafts, games, and exhibits.
www.springfieldvt.com/apple-festival.htm

Vermont Dairy Festival, Enosburg Falls

Visitors have been enjoying the long weekend of shows, parades, and dairy exhibits for more than forty-five years.
www.allarts.org/dairy.htm

Vermont Festival of the Arts, Mad River Valley

More than one hundred art-related events including exhibits, films, performances, and presentations take place over a three-week period in the Mad River Valley.
www.vermontartfest.com

Vermont Maple Festival, St. Albans

The festival includes contests, sugar house tours, carnival rides, and — of course — pancake breakfasts.
www.vtmaplefestival.org

Vermont Mozart Festival, Burlington

For more than thirty years, the music of the famed composer has been celebrated with a summer season of concerts.
www.vtmozart.com

Vermont Quilt Festival, Northfield

Over the past twenty-five years, this exhibit has kept growing. It now includes workshops, classes, and a variety of vendors.
www.vqf.org

Vermont Renaissance Festival, Brattleboro

An English village from the sixteenth century is recreated with actors, musicians, food, and games.
www.vtrenfest.com

Vermont State Fair, Rutland

Held in late August and early September, the State Fair is a ten-day event featuring rides, live entertainment, and agricultural exhibits and games for the whole family.
www.rutlandherald.com/vermontstatefair

Vermont Symphony Orchestra's Summer Tour, various locations

Vermont's sixty-piece orchestra takes to the road for two weeks in late June for a series of outdoor concerts that often end with a spectacular fireworks display.
www.vso.org

▼ The works of composer Wolfgang Amadeus Mozart are celebrated each year in Burlington.

Books

Cheney, Cora. *Vermont: The State with the Storybook Past*. Shelburne, VT: New England Press, 1996. Historical events, both major and minor, fill this readable history of Vermont.

Hahn, Michael T. *Ann Story: Vermont's Heroine of Independence*. Shelburne, VT: New England Press, 1996. The tale of the Vermont heroine who gained fame as "the mother of the Green Mountain Boys."

Hahn, Michael T. *Ethan Allen: A Life of Adventure*. Shelburne, VT: New England Press, 1994. A biography of the complex man who shaped Vermont.

Heinrichs, Ann. *Vermont*. New York: Children's Press, 2001. The lush story of Vermont told in lively 144-page text and brilliant color images.

Kummer, Patricia K. *Vermont (One Nation)*. Mankato, MN: Capstone Press, 1999. The exciting story of the early Republic of Vermont.

Web Sites

▶ Official state web site
www.state.vt.us

▶ Vermont Department of Tourism
www.travel-vermont.com

▶ Official web site of Montpelier, Vermont's capital
www.montpelier-vt.org

▶ Vermont Historical Society
www.state.vt.us/vhs

▶ Vermont: Green Mountain State
www.kidskonnect.com/Vermont/VermontHome.html

Note: Page numbers in *italics* refer to maps, illustrations, or photographs.